The Best Ke Cooker Reci...

The cookbook to eat well and save time.
Low-Carb Recipes for Everyday Dishes.
Improve your body and lose weight.

Odessa Renner

Additionally, the information in the following pages is intended only for informational purposes and should thus be thought of as universal. As befitting its nature, it is presented without assurance regarding its prolonged validity or interim quality. Trademarks that are mentioned are done without written consent and can in no way be considered an endorsement from the trademark holder.

Table of Contents

Introduction

Slow cookers can be really useful in the kitchen and can make life so much easier. They make it so that you can prep your ingredients the day before, and they will be ready for you when you get home. The slow cooker is also great for people on a tight budget, because it can save you a lot of money in the long run. That said, it's important to know how to use your slow cooker properly. Here are some tips to help you get started.

Cook With Low Heat

Always start with low heat when cooking your ingredients in a slow cooker. If you put them over medium heat, they will burn or scorch before they are finished. Instead, start out on low heat and let them cook for several hours until they are done. This will ensure that they are safe to eat and don't have any nasty flavors left over from being cooked too fast.

Leave room at the top

Place your ingredients in the cooker as soon as possible after placing them on the stove top or in the oven. This will give them enough time to cook properly without being overcooked on high heat. If you leave them sitting in the hot pot without food inside of it, sometimes it can become stuck and won't release until you turn off the burner. This can cause some parts of your dish to be overcooked, which can ruin everything you worked so hard to perfect!

Use recipes right away

A great way to use your slow cooker is by developing some new recipes! Have fun experimenting and working on some new ones all at once without having to worry about any nasty flavors ruining your dish later on. Take note of what works well and what does not, so you end up with something delicious every time!

Slow Cookers are a great way to prepare your food and make it taste like someone else has done it for you. With the right recipe in your slow cooker, you can turn days of cooking into hours of preparation.

We've decided to share with you some of our favorite slow cooker recipes from around the country. Some recipes are classic favorites, while others are new and fresh. Whatever you're looking for, you'll find it here.

Slow cookers are a great way to prepare all kinds of meals. With the right recipe, you can cook a variety of dishes, including soups that will warm you up on a cold day.

Some of the advantages to using a slow cooker include reducing the amount of energy needed to use your electric stove. You also don't have to worry about burning yourself when using the stove. You can also leave the slow cooker on when you're not home, making it easy to prepare simple meals and snacks for your family.

You can find many recipes in our slow cooker cookbook. It's divided into several sections, including breakfast, main dishes, side dishes, desserts, and drinks. The slow cooker cookbook is designed for a number of different uses. For example, you can use it to make lots of different side dishes and desserts while you're on vacation or traveling. You can also use the same cookbook in your kitchen to prepare healthy main meals during the week or when you're having friends over for dinner.

Don't let your slow cooker get rusty with age! Contact us today to order our slow cooker cookbook at our guaranteed lowest price. We'll even ship it right away so that you can get started cooking immediately!

Appetizers & Snacks

Candied Walnuts

Preparation time: 15 minutes

Cooking time: 2 hours & 30 minutes

Servings: 16

Ingredients

- ½ cup unsalted butter
- 1-pound walnuts
- ½ cup Splenda, granular
- 1½ teaspoons ground cinnamon
- ¼ teaspoon ground allspice
- ¼ teaspoon ground ginger
- 1/8 teaspoon ground cloves

Directions:

1 Set a slow cooker on high and preheat for about 15 minutes. Add butter and walnuts and stir to combine.

2 Add the Splenda and stir to combine well. Cook, covered, for about 15 minutes.

3 Uncover the slow cooker and stir the mixture. Set to cook on low, uncovered, within 2 hours, stirring occasionally.

4 Transfer the walnuts to a bowl. In another small bowl, mix spices.

5 Sift spice mixture over walnuts and toss to coat evenly. Set aside to cool before serving.

Nutrition:

Calories: 227

Carbohydrates: 10.5g

Protein: 6.9g

Fat: 22.5g

Sugar: 7g

Sodium: 42mg

Fiber: 2.1g

Flavorful Pecans

Preparation time: 15 minutes

Cooking time: 2 hours & 30 minutes

Servings: 16

Ingredients

- 1-pound pecan halves
- ¼ cup butter, melted
- 1 teaspoon dried oregano
- 1 teaspoon dried basil
- 1 teaspoon dried thyme
- 1 tablespoon red chili powder
- ½ teaspoon onion powder
- ¼ teaspoon garlic powder
- ¼ teaspoon cayenne pepper
- Salt, to taste

Directions:

1. Combine all fixings in a large slow cooker.
2. Cook in the slow cooker on high and cook, covered, for about 15 minutes.
3. Uncover the slow cooker and stir the mixture.
4. Cook on low, uncovered, within 2 hours, mixing occasionally.

5 Transfer the pecans into a bowl and keep aside to cool before serving.

Nutrition:

Calories: 225

Carbohydrates: 4.5g

Protein: 3.2g

Fat: 23.2g

Sugar: 1.1g

Sodium: 37mg

Fiber: 3.3g

Herb Flavored Almonds

Preparation time: 15 minutes

Cooking time: 2 hours

Servings: 16

Ingredients

- 2 cups of raw almonds
- 1 tablespoon olive oil
- 1 tablespoon dried rosemary
- 1 tablespoon dried thyme
- Salt
- ground black pepper

Directions:

1 Mix all the fixings in a large slow cooker.

2 Cook in the slow cooker on high and cook, covered, for about 1½ hours, stirring after every 30 minutes. Cool before serving.

Nutrition:

Calories: 77

Carbohydrates: 2.8g

Protein: 2.5g

Fat: 6.9g

Sugar: 0.5g

Sodium: 12mg

Fiber: 1.6g

Ultra-Spicy Almonds

Preparation time: 15 minutes

Cooking time: 2 hours & 30 minutes

Servings: 32

Ingredients

- 2½ tablespoons coconut oil
- cups of raw almonds
- garlic cloves, minced

- 1 teaspoon smoked paprika
- 2 teaspoons red chili powder
- 1 teaspoon ground cumin
- 1 teaspoon onion powder
- Salt
- ground black pepper

Directions:

1 Set a slow cooker on high and preheat for about 25 minutes.
2 Add all Ingredients and stir to combine.
3 Cook on low, uncovered, for about 2 hours, stirring occasionally.
4 Then, in high and cook, uncovered, within 30 minutes.
5 Cool before serving.

Nutrition:

Calories: 80

Carbohydrates: 2.9g

Protein: 2.6g

Fat: 7.1g

Sugar: 0.6g

Sodium: 6mg

Fiber: 1.6g

Tastier Nuts Combo

Preparation time: 15 minutes

Cooking time: 2 hours

Servings: 32

Ingredients

- 1 cup hazelnuts, toasted and skins removed
- 1 cup whole almonds, toasted
- 1 cup pecan halves, toasted
- 1 cup whole cashews
- ½ cup Erythritol
- 1/3 cup butter, melted
- ½ teaspoon ground cinnamon
- ½ teaspoon ground ginger
- ¼ teaspoon ground cloves
- ¼ teaspoon cayenne pepper

Directions:

1 In a large slow cooker, add all fixings and stir to combine.

2 Set on low, covered, cook for about 2 hours, stirring once after 1 hour.

3 Uncover the slow cooker and stir nuts again.

4 Transfer nuts onto a sheet of buttered foil to cool for at least 1 hour before serving.

Nutrition:

Calories: 101

Carbohydrates: 3.1g

Protein: 2.1g

Fat: 0.6g

Sugar: 0.6g

Sodium: 14mg

Fiber: 1.2g

Zesty Chicken Wings

Preparation time: 15 minutes

Cooking time: 7 hours & 12 minutes

Servings: 8

Ingredients

- For Sauce:
- ¼ cup low-sodium soy sauce
- ¼ cup fresh lime juice
- tablespoons Erythritol
- 1 teaspoon Sriracha
- 1 teaspoon ginger powder
- 2 garlic cloves, minced
- 1 teaspoon fresh lime zest, grated finely
- For Wings:
- 2 pounds grass-fed chicken wings
- teaspoons arrowroot starch
- 1 tablespoon water

Directions:

1 For the sauce: Put all sauce fixings in a large bowl, and beat until well combined.
2 Put chicken wings at the bottom of a slow cooker, and top with sauce evenly.

3 Set on low setting and cook, covered, for about 6-7 hours.

4 Dissolve arrowroot starch in water in a small bowl.

5 Uncover the slow cooker and stir in arrowroot mixture until well combined.

6 Cook on high, covered, for about 10-12 minutes.

7 Serve immediately.

Nutrition:

Calories: 456

Carbohydrates: 12.6g

Protein: 66.8g

Fat: 16.9g

Sugar: 8.6g

Sodium: 1084mg

Fiber: 0.2g

Buffalo Chicken Meatballs

Preparation time: 15 minutes

Cooking time: 2 hours & 5 minutes

Servings: 4

Ingredients

- 1-pound ground grass-fed chicken
- 1 organic egg
- 1/3 cup almond meal
- scallions, sliced thinly
- 2 garlic cloves, minced
- Salt
- black pepper, ground
- ¾ cup sugar-free buffalo sauce

Directions:

1. Preheat the oven to 400 degrees F.
2. In a bowl, add all Ingredients except buffalo sauce and mix until well combined.
3. Make 1½-inch balls from chicken mixture.
4. Arrange meatballs onto a baking sheet and bake for about 5 minutes.
5. Remove from oven and transfer meatballs into a slow cooker with buffalo sauce, stir.
6. Cook on low, then covered, for about 2 hours. Serve immediately.

Nutrition:

Calories: 283

Carbohydrates: 3g

Protein: 36.1g

Fat: 13.5g

Sugar: 0.6g

Sodium: 224mg

Fiber: 1.2g

Foolproof Beef Meatballs

Preparation time: 15 minutes

Cooking time: 7 hours & 5 minutes

Servings: 8

Ingredients

- pounds ground lean grass-fed beef
- 2 organic eggs, beaten
- 1 medium yellow onion, chopped
- 2 garlic cloves, minced
- ¼ cup fresh parsley leaves, chopped
- ½ teaspoon red pepper flakes, crushed
- ¼ teaspoon cayenne pepper
- Salt
- ground black pepper
- 2 tablespoons olive oil

Directions:

1. Mix all items except oil in a bowl. Make desired size balls from the mixture.
2. Heat-up oil over medium-high heat in a large skillet, then cook meatballs for 4-5 minutes or until golden brown from all sides.
3. Transfer the meatballs into a greased slow cooker.

4   Cook in the slow cooker on low, covered, for about 7
    hours. Serve hot.

Nutrition:

Calories: 264

Carbohydrates: 10.8g

Protein: 36.1g

Fat: 11.7g

Sugar: 0.7g

Sodium: 508mg

Fiber: 0g

Super-Tasty Pork Meatballs

Preparation time: 15 minutes

Cooking time: 6 hours & 20 minutes

Servings: 8

Ingredients

- pounds lean ground pork
- 1 cup Cheddar cheese, shredded
- 1 large organic egg
- ¼ cup yellow onion, chopped
- ¼ teaspoon ground allspice
- 1 tablespoon water
- tablespoons unsalted butter
- 1½ cups heavy whipping cream
- 1½ cups homemade chicken broth
- 1 tablespoon Worcestershire sauce
- 1 tablespoon Dijon mustard

Directions:

1 Warm-up, the oven to 400 degrees F, then line a large baking dish with parchment paper.

2 In a large bowl, add ground pork, cheddar cheese, egg, onion, allspice, and water and mix until well combined.

3 Make 1½-inch balls from pork mixture.

4   Arrange the meatballs onto a prepared baking dish and bake for about 20 minutes.

5   Meanwhile, in a small skillet, add butter, heavy cream, and broth and bring to a gentle boil over medium heat.

6   Adjust to low and simmer for about 20 minutes, stirring occasionally.

7   Stir in Worcestershire sauce and mustard and remove from heat.

8   In a slow cooker, add sauce and meatballs and stir.

9   Cook in the slow cooker on low, covered, for about 4-6 hours. Serve immediately.

Nutrition:

Calories: 358

Carbohydrates: 1.9g

Protein: 29.2g

Fat: 25.8g

Sugar: 0.8g

Sodium: 398mg

Fiber: 0.2g

Inspiring Sausage Sliders

Preparation time: 15 minutes

Cooking time: 5 hours

Servings: 10

Ingredients

- cups sugar-free ketchup
- ¼ cup Erythritol
- 1 tablespoon Worcestershire sauce
- 2 teaspoons mustard
- 1 teaspoon hot sauce
- 1 medium yellow onion, chopped finely
- ½ cup homemade chicken broth
- 2 pounds pork sausage, cut into ½-inch rounds

Directions:

1 In a large slow cooker, add all items and stir to combine.
2 Cook on low, covered, for about 4-5 hours.
3 Serve immediately.

Nutrition:

Calories: 365

Carbohydrates: 13.7g

Protein: 19g

Fat: 26.2g

Sugar: 11.8g

Sodium: 1280mg

Fiber: 0.5g

Potluck Party Peppers

Preparation time: 15 minutes

Cooking time: 9 hours

Servings: 10

Ingredients

- 1½ pounds mini sweet peppers, seeded and tops removed
- 1-pound ground Italian sausage
- 1 (24-ounce) jar sugar-free spaghetti sauce
- 8-ounce mozzarella cheese, shredded

Directions:

1 Stuff each pepper evenly with sausage.
2 Lightly greased slow cooker, arrange peppers. Cook on low, covered, for about 6-8 hours.
3 Uncover the slow cooker and top each pepper with mozzarella cheese.
4 Cook, covered for about 10 minutes. Serve hot.

Nutrition:

Calories: 248

Carbohydrates: 9.6g

Protein: 15.6g

Fat: 16g

Sugar: 7.5g

Sodium: 824mg

Fiber: 1.8g

Perfect Eggplant Tapenade

Preparation time: 15 minutes

Cooking time: 9 hours

Servings: 2

Ingredients

- cups eggplants, chopped
- 1 cup tomatoes, chopped
- garlic cloves, minced
- 2 teaspoons capers
- 2 teaspoons fresh lemon juice
- 1 teaspoon dried basil
- Salt, to taste
- Pinch of ground black pepper

Directions:

1 In a slow cooker, add eggplant, tomatoes, garlic, and capers and mix well.
2 Cook on low, covered, for about 7-9 hours.
3 Uncover the slow cooker and stir in the remaining Ingredients
4 Serve hot.

Nutrition:

Calories: 46

Carbohydrates: 10.1g

Protein: 2g

Fat: 0.4g

Sugar: 5g

Sodium: 170mg

Fiber: 4.2g

Swiss Style Cheese Fondue

Preparation time: 15 minutes

Cooking time: 3 hours & 10 minutes

Servings: 6

Ingredients

- 1 clove garlic, cut in half
- 2½ cups homemade chicken broth
- tablespoons fresh lemon juice
- 16 ounces Swiss cheese, shredded
- ounces Cheddar cheese, shredded
- tablespoons almond flour
- Pinch of ground nutmeg
- Pinch of paprika

- Pinch of ground black pepper

Directions:

1. Rub a pan evenly with cut garlic halves. Add broth and place pan over medium heat.
2. Cook until mixture is just beginning to bubble. Adjust to low, then stir in lemon juice.
3. Meanwhile, in a bowl, mix cheeses and flour. Slowly, add cheese mixture to broth, stirring continuously.
4. Cook until cheese mixture becomes thick, stirring continuously. Transfer the cheese mixture to a greased slow cooker and sprinkle with nutmeg, paprika, and black pepper.
5. Cook in the slow cooker on low, covered, for about 1-3 hours.

Nutrition:

Calories: 479

Carbohydrates: 6.1g

Protein: 32.6g

Fat: 36g

Sugar: 1.8g

Sodium: 700mg

Fiber: 0.5g

Tex-Mex Cheese Dip

Preparation time: 15 minutes

Cooking time: 1 hour & 30 minutes

Servings: 6

Ingredients

- ounces Velveeta cheese, cubed
- ¾ cup diced tomatoes with green chili peppers
- 1 teaspoon taco seasoning

Directions:

1 In a slow cooker, place Velveeta cheese cubes.

2 Cook on low and cook, covered, for about 30-60 minutes, stirring occasionally.

3 Uncover the slow cooker and stir in tomatoes and taco seasoning. Cook, covered, for about 30 minutes

4 Serve hot.

Nutrition:

Calories: 114

Carbohydrates: 5.2g

Protein: 7g

Fat: 8.1g

Sugar: 3.4g

Sodium: 577mg

Fiber: 0.3g

2-Ingredient Cheese Dip

Preparation time: 15 minutes

Cooking time: 2 hours

Servings: 20

Ingredients

- 16 ounces Velveeta cheese, cubed
- 1 (16-ounce) jar salsa

Directions:

1 In a large slow cooker, place cheese and salsa and stir gently to combine.
2 Cook on high, covered, for about 2 hours, stirring occasionally. Serve hot.

Nutrition:

Calories: 71

Carbohydrates: 3.9g

Protein: 4.4g

Fat: 4.9g

Sugar: 2.3g

Sodium: 460mg

Fiber: 0.4g

Asparagus Bacon Bouquet

Preparation time: 15 minutes

Cooking time: 4 hours

Servings: 4

Ingredients

- asparagus spears, trimmed
- slices bacon
- 1 tsp black pepper
- Extra virgin olive oil

Directions:

1 Coat slow cooker with extra virgin olive oil.

2 Slice spears in half, and sprinkle with black pepper

3 Wrap three spear halves with one slice bacon, and set inside the slow cooker.

4 Cook for 4 hours on medium.

Nutrition:

Calories 345

Carbs 2 g

Fat 27 g

Protein 22 g

Sodium 1311 mg

Sugar 0 g

Creamy Asiago Spinach Dip

Preparation time: 15 minutes

Cooking time: 4 hours

Servings: 6

Ingredients

- cups spinach, wash, chopped
- ½ cup artichoke hearts
- ½ cup cream cheese
- ½ cup Asiago cheese, grated
- ½ cup almond milk
- 1 tsp black pepper
- Extra virgin olive oil

Directions:

1 Coat slow cooker with olive oil.

2 Place cream cheese and almond milk in a blender, and mix until smooth.

3 Finely chop spinach, add to blender along with salt and black pepper, and mix.

4 Place spinach mixture in a blender, add artichoke hearts and mix in with a spatula.

5 Sprinkle Asiago cheese on top, and cook on medium for 4 hours.

6 Serve dip with a selection of veggies like broccoli florets and carrot sticks.

Nutrition:

Calories 214

Carbs 4 g

Fat 19 g

Protein 8 g

Sodium 380 mg

Sugar 1 g

Madras Curry Chicken Bites

Preparation time: 15 minutes

Cooking time: 7 hours

Servings: 4

Ingredients

- 1 lb. chicken breasts, skinless, boneless
- cloves garlic, grated
- 1 tsp ginger, grated
- 2 cups low-sodium chicken stock
- 2 lemons, juiced
- 1 tsp coriander, crushed
- 1 tsp cumin
- ½ tsp fenugreek
- 1 tbsp. curry powder
- ½ tsp cinnamon
- 1½ tsp salt
- 1 tsp black pepper
- Extra virgin olive oil

Directions:

1 Cube chicken breast into ½" pieces, and sprinkle with ½ tsp salt and ½ tsp black pepper.

2 Heat 3 tbsp. extra virgin olive oil in a skillet, add chicken breasts, and brown.

3 Place chicken breasts in a slow cooker.

4 Add chicken stock, garlic, lemon juice, spices, and salt.

5 Cook on low for 7 hours.

Nutrition:

Calories 234

Carbs 3 g

Fat 8 g

Protein 38 g

Sodium 782 mg

Sugar 0 g

Spiced Jicama Wedges with Cilantro Chutney

Preparation time: 15 minutes

Cooking time: 4 hours

Servings: 8

Ingredients

- 1 lb. jicama, peeled
- 1 tsp paprika
- ½ tsp dried parsley
- 2 tsp salt
- 2 tsp black pepper
- Extra virgin olive oil
- Cilantro Chutney
- 1 tsp dill chopped
- ¼ cup cilantro
- ½ tsp salt
- 1 tsp paprika
- 1tsp black pepper
- 2 lemons, juiced
- ¼ cup extra virgin olive oil

Directions:

1 Slice jicama into 1" wedges, and submerge in a bowl of cold water for 20 minutes.
2 Place the paprika, oregano, salt, black pepper in a bowl, and toss with jicama.
3 Add 5 tbsp. extra virgin olive oil into a bowl and coat well.
4 Place jicama in the slow cooker, and cook on high for 4 hours.

5 Combine Ingredients for chutney in blender, mix, and refrigerate until jicama wedges are ready to serve.

Nutrition:

Calories 94

Carbs 5.2 g

Fat 8 g

Protein 1 g

Sodium 879 mg

Sugar 1 g

Teriyaki Chicken Wings

Preparation time: 15 minutes

Cooking time: 4 hours

Servings: 4

Ingredients:

- 2 lb. chicken wings
- 2 tsp ginger, grated
- cloves garlic, grated
- ¼ cup of soy sauce
- dates, pitted
- Extra virgin olive oil

Directions

1. Processed the dates in a food processor along with 2 tbsp. soy sauce, and mix until pasty.
2. Combine ginger, garlic, soy sauce, and dates in a bowl, add chicken wings, coat, and refrigerate overnight.
3. Coat slow cooker with a little sesame oil, add chicken wings and cook on high for 4 hours.

Nutrition:

Calories 354

Carbs 5.5 g

Fat 16 g

Protein 45 g

Sodium 730 mg

Sugar 0 g

Portabella Pizza Bites

Preparation time: 15 minutes

Cooking time: 5 hours

Servings: 8

Ingredients

- Portabella Mushrooms
- ½ lb. ground pork
- 1 medium onion, diced
- cloves garlic, grated
- 2 cups crushed tomato
- ½ cup Mozzarella, shredded
- ¼ cup Parmesan
- ½ tsp oregano
- 1 tsp salt
- 1 tsp black pepper
- Garnish
- ½ cup parsley, chopped

Directions:

1. Coat 6 qt. slow cooker with extra virgin olive oil
2. Heat 3 tbsp. extra virgin olive oil in a skillet, add pork, brown.
3. Mix crushed tomato with salt, black pepper, oregano, parmesan, and garlic.

4   Spoon a little tomato-parmesan mixture into each mushroom, add a little ground pork, and sprinkle with Mozzarella.

5   Place each mushroom in a slow cooker. Cook pizza bites on medium for 5 hours.

6   Sprinkle a little parsley on top before serving.

Nutrition:

Calories 106

Carbs 5.6 g

Fat 3 g

Protein 13 g

Sodium 421 mg

Sugar 2 g

Garlic Parmesan Chicken Wings

Preparation time: 10 Minutes

Cooking time: 3 Hours 20 Minutes

Servings: 8

Ingredients

- 1 cup Parmesan Cheese, shredded
- lb. Chicken Wings
- ¼ tsp. Black Pepper, grounded
- ½ cup Butter, preferably organic

- 1 tsp. Sea Salt
- Garlic cloves, finely minced

Directions:

1 Begin by placing the chicken wings in the bottom portion of the slow cooker. After that, butter a large skillet over medium heat, and to this, add the garlic.

2 Sauté the garlic for 30 to 50 seconds or until aromatic. Spoon in the oil over the chicken wings and coat them well.

3 Now, cook them for 3 hours on low heat. Toward the end time, preheat the oven to broil.

4 Line the baking sheet using a parchment paper. Once the chicken is cooked, transfer them to the baking sheet in a single layer.

5 Broil it within 5 minutes or until the chicken is golden brown in color and crispy. Bring the baking sheet out after 5 minutes and top it with the cheese.

6 Return the sheet to oven and bake for another 2 minutes or until melted.

Nutrition:

Calories: 426

Fat: 34g

Carbohydrates: 1g

Proteins: 27g

Candied Pecans

Preparation time: 5 Minutes

Cooking time: 3 Hours

Servings: 12

Ingredients

- 1 cup Sukrin Gold
- 1 Egg White, medium-sized
- cups Pecan
- ¼ cup Water
- tsp. Vanilla Extract
- 1 ½ tbsp. Cinnamon

Directions:

1 First, butter the insides of the slow cooker and transfer the pecans to it.
2 After that, mix vanilla extract and egg white in a mixing bowl until just combined and foamy.
3 Spoon this egg mixture over the pan. Stir them so that they coat the pecans well. Now, combine the cinnamon with the Sukrin Gold until well incorporated.
4 Pour the batter over the pecans and stir them again.
5 Then, close the lid and cook for 3 hours on low heat while stirring them every quarter of an hour.

6   Once the time is up, transfer the pecans to a baking sheet in a single layer and allow it to cool. Serve and enjoy.

Nutrition:

Calories: 257

Fat: 26g

Carbohydrates: 4g

Proteins: 4g

Cocoa Nuts

Preparation time: 5 Minutes

Cooking time: 1 Hour

Servings: 6

Ingredients

- ½ cup Walnuts
- tbsp. Swerve
- ½ cup Almonds, slivered
- tbsp. Butter softened
- ½ cup Pecans, halved
- 2 tbsp. Cocoa Powder, unsweetened
- 1 tsp. Vanilla Extract

Directions:

1 First, place all the Ingredients needed to make this snack in a large mixing bowl. Mix well until well combined.

2 Transfer the nut mixture to the slow cooker—Cook within 1 hour on high heat.

3 Once the cooking time is up, place them on a baking sheet and cool before storing.

Nutrition:

Calories: 218

Fat: 21g

Carbohydrates: 2g

Proteins: 4g

Thai Curry Nuts

Preparation time: 5 Minutes

Cooking time: 1 Hour & 30 Minutes

Servings: 8

Ingredients

- cups Nuts, raw
- ½ tsp. Salt
- ¼ cup Coconut Oil
- 1 tbsp. Curry Paste
- 1 tbsp. Swerve Sweetener

Directions:

1 Start by heating the slow cooker to high heat. Add coconut oil to slow cooker and once the oil has melted, stir in curry paste, salt, and sugar. Mix well.

2 Once the spice paste has dissolved, add the raw nuts. Stir them well so that the syrup coats the nuts well. Then, cover the lid and cook for 1 ½ hour on high heat.

3 Finally, transfer the nuts to a baking sheet and allow them to cool completely before storing.

Nutrition:

Calories: 547

Fat: 57g

Carbohydrates: 5g

Proteins: 5.41g

Pumpkin Spiced Nuts

Preparation time: 15 Minutes

Cooking time: 2 Hours

Servings: 4

Ingredients

- 1 cup Walnuts, raw & halved
- Egg Whites, large
- cups Almonds, raw & unsalted

- 1 ½ tbsp. Pumpkin Pie Spice
- 2 cups Cashews, raw & unsalted
- 1 cup Brazil Nuts, raw & unsalted
- 1 ½ cup Coconut Sugar

Directions:

1 First, grease the insides of the slow cooker with oil or butter.

2 After that, combine the nuts with the pumpkin pie spice and coconut sugar. Mix well.

3 Then, add the egg whites into it until everything comes together. Now, transfer the nut mixture to the slow cooker.

4 Cook for 2 hours on low heat. Make sure to stir them every 45 minutes or so.

5 Once the nuts are done with cooking, place them on a baking sheet and allow it to cool completely.

Nutrition:

Calories: 382

Fat: 34.66g

Carbohydrates: 7g

Proteins: 10.92g

Turkey Meatballs

Preparation time: 15 Minutes

Cooking time: 6 Hours

Servings: 20

Ingredients

- 1lb. Turkey
- Garlic cloves, crushed
- ½ tsp. Onion Powder
- 1 tbsp. Red Wine Vinegar
- ½ tsp. Rosemary
- 1 lb. Turkey sausage, grounded
- 1 Egg, large & organic
- ½ tsp. Thyme
- 1 tsp. Salt
- ½ of 1 Onion, large & diced
- ½ tsp. Garlic powder
- 1 tsp. Basil
- 1 × 28 oz. Can have crushed Tomatoes
- ½ tsp. Oregano
- ½ cup Almond Meal

Directions:

1 First, you need to mix turkey and sausage in a large bowl until well combined.

2 After that, stir together onion powder, basil, almond meal, oregano, garlic powder, and rosemary in another bowl until mixed well.

3 Then, put the almond meal batter to the meat mixture and give everything a good stir.

4 Mix in the egg until well incorporated. Now, form a ball out of this mixture and place them on the baking sheet.

5 Place them in the oven and broil them for 2 to 3 minutes. Once broiled, add the meatballs to the slow cooker.

6 Top the meatballs with garlic, onion, vinegar, tomatoes, and salt.

7 Close the lid and cook them for 6 hours on low heat. Finally, garnish them with basil before serving.

Nutrition:

Calories: 95

Fat: 7.14g

Carbohydrates: 1.85g

Proteins: 10.18g

Bok Choy Brownies

Preparation time: 10 Minutes

Cooking time: 4 Hours

Servings: 8

Ingredients

- 1 packet of Bok Choy, trimmed and stems coarsely chopped
- ½ cup Swerve Sweetener
- Eggs, large & organic
- ½ tsp. Salt
- 1 tsp. Baking powder
- 1 cup Almond Flour
- 1 tsp. Vanilla Extract
- ½ cup Cocoa Powder
- 1/3 cup Coconut Oil
- ½ tsp. Espresso powder

Directions:

1 To begin with, grease the insides of the slow cooker. Heat saltwater in a saucepan over medium heat and place the bok choy into it.

2 Simmer for 5 minutes or until the stems are cooked well.

3   Now, transfer the cooked bok choy to a blender and blend until it becomes a smooth puree. Mix all the dry fixing in a large mixing bowl.

4   Add the wet fixing one by one until everything comes together. Put the batter inside the slow cooker and close the lid.

5   Cook within 4 hours on low heat or until the center is set and a toothpick inserted comes clean.

6   Allow them to cool in the slow cooker itself and then slice them into small pieces. Serve warm or cold.

Nutrition:

Calories: 235

Fat: 20.82g

Carbohydrates: 5.39g

Proteins: 6.68g

Lemon Custard

Preparation time: 10 Minutes

Cooking time: 3 Hours

Servings: 4

Ingredients

- Egg yolks, large & organic
- 1 tsp. Vanilla Extract
- cups Whipping Cream
- 1 tbsp. Lemon zest
- ½ tsp. Liquid Stevia
- ¼ cup Lemon Juice, freshly squeezed

Directions:

1 Combine egg yolks, liquid stevia, lemon juice, and zest and vanilla extract in a medium-sized mixing bowl.

2 Once well combined, add whipping cream to the bowl and stir them again. Divide the mixture into 4 ramekins.

3 After that, place a rack into the slow cooker and arrange the ramekins on it. Put water inside the slow cooker, so it reaches halfway up the sides of the ramekins.

4   Cook within 3 hours on low heat. Finally, remove the ramekins from the slow cooker and allow them to cool at room temperature.

5   Chill them in the refrigerator.

Nutrition:

Calories: 319

Fat: 30g

Carbohydrates: 3g

Proteins: 7g

Buffalo Chicken Dip

Preparation time: 10 Minutes

Cooking time: 2 Hours

Servings: 8

Ingredients

- 1 tbsp. Ranch Seasoning
- cups cooked chicken, diced
- 1 cup Hot Sauce
- oz. Blue Cheese, crumbled
- 1 cup Sour Cream
- ½ cup Green Onion, thinly sliced
- 1 × 8 oz. Cream Cheese, chopped into cubes
- cups Mozzarella Cheese, shredded

Directions:

1 Start by greasing the insides of the slow cooker. Stir in all the remaining **Ingredients:** into the slow cooker and mix well.
2 Cook for 2 hours on high heat or until the cheese is melted. Garnish with green onions and serve it along with celery stalks.

Nutrition:

Calories: 344

Fat: 25.3g

Carbohydrates: 5.3g

Proteins: 22.39g

Side Dish Recipes

Garlic Carrots Mix

Preparation time: 15 minutes

Cooking time: 4 Hours

Servings: 2

Ingredients

- 1 pound carrots, sliced
- 2 garlic cloves, minced
- 1 red onion, chopped
- 1 tablespoon olive oil
- ½ cup tomato sauce
- A pinch of salt and black pepper
- ½ teaspoon oregano, dried
- 2 teaspoons lemon zest, grated
- 1 tablespoon lemon juice
- 1 tablespoon chives, chopped

Directions:

1. In your Crock Pot, mix the carrots with the garlic, onion and then add the other Ingredients, toss, put the lid on and cook on Low for 4 hours.
2. Divide the mix between plates and serve.

Nutrition: calories 219, fat 8, fiber 4, carbs 8, protein 17

Marjoram Rice Mix

Preparation time: 15 minutes

Cooking time: 6 Hours

Servings: 2

Ingredients

- 1 cup wild rice
- 2 cups chicken stock
- 1 carrot, peeled and grated
- 2 tablespoons marjoram, chopped
- 1 tablespoon olive oil
- A pinch of salt and black pepper
- 1 tablespoon green onions, chopped

Directions:

1. In your Crock Pot, mix the rice with the stock and after that add the other Ingredients, toss, put the lid on and cook on Low for 6 hours.

2. Divide between plates and serve.

Nutrition: calories 200, fat 2, fiber 3, carbs 7, protein 5

Green Beans and Mushrooms

Preparation time: 15 minutes

Cooking time: 3 Hours

Servings: 4

Ingredients

- 1 pound fresh green beans, trimmed
- 1 small yellow onion, chopped
- 6 ounces bacon, chopped
- 1 garlic clove, minced

- 1 cup chicken stock
- 8 ounces mushrooms, sliced
- Salt and black pepper to the taste
- A splash of balsamic vinegar

Directions:

1. In your Crock Pot, mix beans with onion, bacon, garlic, stock, mushrooms, salt, pepper and vinegar, stir, cover and cook on Low for 3 hours.

2. Divide between plates and serve as a side dish.

Nutrition: calories 162, fat 4, fiber 5, carbs 8, protein 4

Beans and Red Peppers

Preparation time: 15 minutes

Cooking time: 2 Hrs.

Servings: 2

Ingredients

- 2 cups green beans, halved
- 1 red bell pepper, cut into strips
- Salt and black pepper to the taste
- 1 tbsp. olive oil
- 1 and ½ tbsp. honey mustard

Directions:

1. Add green beans; honey mustard, red bell pepper, oil, salt, and black to Crock Pot.
2. Put on the cooker's lid on and set the cooking time to hours on High settings.
3. Serve warm.

Nutrition: Per Serving: Calories: 50, Total Fat: 0g, Fiber: 4g, Total Carbs: 8g, Protein: 2g

Cabbage and Onion Mix

Preparation time: 15 minutes

Cooking time: 2 Hours

Servings: 2

Ingredients

- 1 and ½ cups green cabbage, shredded
- 1 cup red cabbage, shredded
- 1 tablespoon olive oil
- 1 red onion, sliced
- 2 spring onions, chopped
- ½ cup tomato paste
- ¼ cup veggie stock
- 2 tomatoes, chopped
- 2 jalapenos, chopped
- 1 tablespoon chili powder
- 1 tablespoon chives, chopped
- A pinch of salt and black pepper

Directions:

1. Grease your Crock Pot with the oil and mix the cabbage with the onion, spring onions and the other **Ingredients:** inside.

2.   Toss, put the lid on and cook on High for hours.

3.   Divide between plates and serve as a side dish.

Nutrition: calories 211, fat 3, fiber 3, carbs 6, protein 8

Cauliflower and Potatoes Mix

Preparation time: 15 minutes

Cooking time: 4 Hours

Servings: 2

Ingredients

- 1 cup cauliflower florets
- ½ pound sweet potatoes, peeled and cubed
- 1 cup veggie stock

- ½ cup tomato sauce
- 1 tablespoon chives, chopped
- Salt and black pepper to the taste
- 1 teaspoon sweet paprika

Directions:

1. In your Crock Pot, mix the cauliflower with the potatoes, stock and the other Ingredients, toss, put the lid on and cook on High for 4 hours.
2. Divide between plates and serve as a side dish.

Nutrition: calories 135, fat 5, fiber 1, carbs 7, protein 3

Broccoli Mix

Preparation time: 15 minutes

Cooking time: 2 Hours

Servings: 10

Ingredients

- 6 cups broccoli florets
- 1 and ½ cups cheddar cheese, shredded
- 10 ounces canned cream of celery soup

- ½ teaspoon Worcestershire sauce

- ¼ cup yellow onion, chopped

- Salt and black pepper to the taste

- 1 cup crackers, crushed

- 2 tablespoons soft butter

Directions:

1. In a bowl, mix broccoli with cream of celery soup, cheese, salt, pepper, onion and Worcestershire sauce, toss and transfer to your Crock Pot.

2. Add butter, toss again, sprinkle crackers, cover and cook on High for hours.

3. Serve as a side dish.

Nutrition: calories 159, fat 11, fiber 1, carbs 11, protein 6

Roasted Beets

Preparation time: 15 minutes

Cooking time: 4 Hours

Servings: 5

Ingredients

- 10 small beets
- 5 teaspoons olive oil
- A pinch of salt and black pepper

Directions:

1. Divide each beet on a tin foil piece, drizzle oil, season them with salt and pepper, rub well, wrap beets, place them in your Crock Pot, cover and cook on High for 4 hours.

2. Unwrap beets, cool them down a bit, peel, and slice and serve them as a side dish.

Nutrition: calories 100, fat 2, fiber 2, carbs 4, protein 5

Lemony Pumpkin Wedges

Preparation time: 15 minutes

Cooking time: 6 Hours

Servings: 4

Ingredients

- 15 oz. pumpkin, peeled and cut into wedges
- 1 tbsp. lemon juice
- 1 tsp. salt
- 1 tsp. honey
- ½ tsp. ground cardamom
- 1 tsp. lime juice

Directions:

1. Add pumpkin, lemon juice, honey, lime juice, cardamom, and salt to the Crock Pot.
2. Put the slow cooker's lid on and set the cooking time to 6 hours on Low settings.
3. Serve fresh.

Nutrition: Per Serving: Calories: 35, Total Fat: 0.1g, Fiber: 1g, Total Carbs: 8.91g, Protein: 1g

Thai Side Salad

Preparation time: 15 minutes

Cooking time: 3 Hours

Servings: 8

Ingredients

- 8 ounces yellow summer squash, peeled and roughly chopped
- 12 ounces zucchini, halved and sliced
- 2 cups button mushrooms, quartered
- 1 red sweet potatoes, chopped
- 2 leeks, sliced
- 2 tablespoons veggie stock
- 2 garlic cloves, minced
- 2 tablespoon Thai red curry paste
- 1 tablespoon ginger, grated
- 1/3 cup coconut milk
- ¼ cup basil, chopped

Directions:

1. In your Crock Pot, mix zucchini with summer squash, mushrooms, red pepper, leeks, garlic, stock, curry paste, ginger, coconut milk and basil, toss, cover and cook on Low for 3 hours.
2. Stir your Thai mix one more time, divide between plates and serve as a side dish.

Nutrition: calories 69, fat 2, fiber 2, carbs 8, protein 2

Eggplants with Mayo Sauce

Preparation time: 15 minutes

Cooking time: 5 Hours

Servings: 8

Ingredients

- 2 tbsp. minced garlic
- 1 chili pepper, chopped
- 1 sweet pepper, chopped
- 4 tbsp. mayo
- 1 tsp. olive oil
- 1 tsp. salt
- ½ tsp. ground black pepper
- 18 oz. eggplants, peeled and diced
- 2 tbsp. sour cream

Directions:

1. Blend chili pepper, sweet peppers, salt, garlic, and black pepper in a blender until smooth.
2. Add eggplant and this chili mixture to the Crock Pot then toss them well.
3. Now mix mayo with sour cream and spread on top of eggplants.

4. Put the cooker's lid on and set the cooking time to 5 hours on High settings.

5. Serve warm

Nutrition: Per Serving: Calories: 40, Total Fat: 1.1g, Fiber: 3g, Total Carbs: 7.5g, Protein: 1g

Summer Squash Medley

Preparation time: 15 minutes

Cooking time: 2 hours

Servings: 4

Ingredients

- ¼ cup olive oil
- 2 tbsp. basil, chopped
- 2 tbsp. balsamic vinegar
- 2 garlic cloves, minced
- 2 tsp. mustard
- Salt and black pepper to the taste
- 3 summer squash, sliced
- 2 zucchinis, sliced

Directions:

1. Add squash, zucchinis, and all other **Ingredients:** to the Crock Pot.
2. Put the cooker's lid on and set the cooking time to hours on High settings.
3. Serve.

Nutrition: Per Serving: Calories: 179, Total Fat: 13g, Fiber: 2g, Total Carbs: 10g, Protein: 4g

Garlic Butter Green Beans

Preparation time: 15 minutes

Cooking time: 2 Hours

Servings: 6

Ingredients

- 22 ounces green beans
- 2 garlic cloves, minced
- ¼ cup butter, soft
- 2 tablespoons parmesan, grated

Directions:

1. In your Crock Pot, mix green beans with garlic, butter and parmesan, toss, cover and cook on High for 2 hours.

2. Divide between plates, sprinkle parmesan all over and serve as a side dish.

Nutrition: calories 60, fat 4, fiber 1, carbs 3, protein 1

Green Beans and Red Peppers

Preparation time: 15 minutes

Cooking time: 2 Hours

Servings: 2

Ingredients

- 2 cups green beans, halved
- 1 red bell pepper, cut into strips
- Salt and black pepper to the taste
- 1 tablespoon olive oil
- 1 and ½ tablespoon honey mustard

Directions:

1. In your Crock Pot, mix green beans with bell pepper, salt, pepper, oil and honey mustard, toss, cover and cook on High for 2 hours.
2. Divide between plates and serve as a side dish.

Nutrition: calories 50, fat 0, fiber 4, carbs 8, protein 2

Cauliflower Carrot Gratin

Preparation time: 15 minutes

Cooking time: 7 Hours

Servings: 12

Ingredients

- 16 oz. baby carrots
- 6 tbsp. butter, soft
- 1 cauliflower head, florets separated
- Salt and black pepper to the taste
- 1 yellow onion, chopped
- 1 tsp. mustard powder
- 1 and ½ cups of milk
- 6 oz. cheddar cheese, grated
- ½ cup breadcrumbs

Directions:

1. Add carrots, cauliflower, and rest of the **Ingredients:** to the Crock Pot.
2. Put the cooker's lid on and set the cooking time to 7 hours on Low settings.
3. Serve warm.

Nutrition: Per Serving: Calories: 182, Total Fat: 4g, Fiber: 7g, Total Carbs: 9g, Protein: 4g

Minty Peas and Tomatoes

Preparation time: 15 minutes

Cooking time: 3 Hours

Servings: 2

Ingredients

- 1 pound okra, sliced
- ½ pound tomatoes, cut into wedges
- 1 tablespoon olive oil
- ½ cup veggie stock
- ½ teaspoon chili powder
- Salt and black pepper to the taste
- 1 tablespoon mint, chopped
- 3 green onions, chopped
- 1 tablespoon chives, chopped

Directions:

1. Grease your Crock Pot with the oil, and mix the okra with the tomatoes and the other **Ingredients:** inside.

2. Put the lid on, cook on Low for 3 hours, divide between plates and serve as a side dish.

Nutrition: calories 70, fat 1, fiber 1, carbs 4, protein 6

Lemon Artichokes

Preparation time: 15 minutes

Cooking time: 3 Hours

Servings: 2

Ingredients

- 1 cup veggie stock
- 2 medium artichokes, trimmed
- 1 tablespoon lemon juice
- 1 tablespoon lemon zest, grated
- Salt to the taste

Directions:

1. In your Crock Pot, mix the artichokes with the stock and the other Ingredients, and then toss it, put the lid on and cook on Low for 3 hours.

2. Divide artichokes between plates and serve as a side dish.

Nutrition: calories 100, fat 2, fiber 5, carbs 10, protein 4

Mashed Potatoes

Preparation time: 15 minutes

Cooking time: 6 Hours

Servings: 2

Ingredients

- 1 pound gold potatoes, peeled and cubed
- 2 garlic cloves, chopped
- 1 cup milk
- 1 cup water
- 2 tablespoons butter

- A pinch of salt and white pepper

Directions:

1. In your Crock Pot, mix the potatoes with the water, salt and pepper, put the lid on and cook on Low for 6 hours.

2. Mash the potatoes; add the rest of the Ingredients, whisk and serve.

Nutrition: calories 135, fat 4, fiber 2, carbs 10, protein 4

Jalapeno Meal

Preparation time: 15 minutes

Cooking time: 6 Hrs.

Servings: 6

Ingredients

- 12 oz. jalapeno pepper, cut in half and deseeded
- 2 tbsp. olive oil
- 1 tbsp. balsamic vinegar
- 1 onion, sliced
- 1 garlic clove, sliced
- 1 tsp. ground coriander
- 4 tbsp. water

Directions:

1. Place the jalapeno peppers in the Crock Pot.
2. Top the pepper with olive oil, balsamic vinegar, onion, garlic, coriander, and water.
3. Put the cooker's lid on and set the cooking time to 6 hours on Low settings.
4. Serve warm.

Nutrition: Per Serving: Calories: 67, Total Fat: 4.7g, Fiber: 2g, Total Carbs: 6.02g, Protein: 1g

Blueberry Spinach Salad

Preparation time: 15 minutes

Cooking time: 1 Hour

Servings: 3

Ingredients

- ¼ cup pecans, chopped
- ½ tsp. sugar
- 2 tsp. maple syrup
- 1 tbsp. white vinegar
- 2 tbsp. orange juice
- 1 tbsp. olive oil
- 4 cups spinach
- 2 oranges, peeled and cut into segments
- 1 cup blueberries

Directions:

1. Add pecans, maple syrup, and rest of the **Ingredients:** to the Crock Pot.
2. Put the cooker's lid on and set the cooking time to 1 hour on High settings.
3. Serve warm.

Nutrition: Per Serving: Calories: 140, Total Fat: 4g, Fiber: 3g, Total Carbs: 10g, Protein: 3g

Dill Mixed Fennel

Preparation time: 15 minutes

Cooking time: 3 Hour

Servings: 7

Ingredients

- 10 oz. fennel bulbs, diced
- 2 tbsp. olive oil
- 1 tsp. ground black pepper
- 1 tsp. paprika
- 1 tsp. cilantro
- 1 tsp. oregano
- 1 tsp. basil
- 3 tbsp. white wine
- 1 tsp. salt
- 2 garlic cloves
- 1 tsp. dried dill

Directions:

1. Add fennel bulbs and all other **Ingredients:** to the Crock Pot.
2. Put the cooker's lid on and set the cooking time to 3.5 hours on High settings.
3. Serve warm.

Nutrition: Per Serving: Calories: 53, Total Fat: 4.1g, Fiber: 2g, Total Carbs: 4g, Protein: 1g

Okra and Corn

Preparation time: 15 minutes

Cooking time: 8 Hours

Servings: 4

Ingredients

- 3 garlic cloves, minced
- 1 small green bell pepper, chopped
- 1 small yellow onion, chopped
- 1 cup water
- 16 ounces okra, sliced
- 2 cups corn
- 1 and ½ teaspoon smoked paprika
- 28 ounces canned tomatoes, crushed
- 1 teaspoon oregano, dried
- 1 teaspoon thyme, dried
- 1 teaspoon marjoram, dried
- A pinch of cayenne pepper
- Salt and black pepper to the taste

Directions:

1. In your Crock Pot, mix garlic with bell pepper, onion, water, okra, corn, paprika, tomatoes, oregano, thyme, marjoram, cayenne, salt and pepper, cover, cook on Low for 8 hours, divide between plates and serve as a side dish.

Nutrition: calories 182, fat 3, fiber 6, carbs 8, protein 5

CPSIA information can be obtained
at www.ICGtesting.com
Printed in the USA
BVHW051756120421
604747BV00011B/762

9 781801 831291